Cow in a Crash Helmet

Written by
Pauline Tucker

Illustrated by

Basil Waite

Myrtle's Mishaps Book 1
Onion Custard Kids

Cow in a Crash Helmet
Myrtle's Mishaps: Book 1

© 2020 Pauline Tucker
© Cover illustration by Basil Waite
Cover design © 2020 David Norrington

British Library Cataloguing in Publication Data.
A catalogue record for this book is available from the British Library.

Published in the UK by Onion Custard Kids,
an imprint of Wordcatcher Publishing Group Ltd
www.wordcatcher.com
Tel: 02921 888321

First Edition: 2020

Print edition ISBN: 9781789422542
Ebook edition ISBN: 9781789423075

Category: Children's Fiction 4-7 years

Myrtle's Motorbike

For as long as she could remember, Myrtle had wanted a motorbike. The field she lived in was next to a road and she loved to watch the motorbikes as they roared past the gate and around the corner.

Myrtle decided to save some money until she had enough to buy the bike of her dreams. *I must get a shiny new helmet and some gloves as well*, she thought.

In the orchard behind the farmhouse were some other cows who had just had babies. Myrtle wandered across and popped her head over the fence.

"You must be exhausted, looking after your calves all day," she said. "I could look after them while you have a rest or go for a walk."

The cows thought this was a fantastic idea and readily agreed.

Myrtle hoped she could keep all the money she made from her new job. If she saved hard, she might have enough to buy a motorbike of her own.

The farmer looked out through his kitchen window and saw the cows from the orchard walking past. He leapt to his feet and ran into the yard, thinking they had escaped and left their calves all alone.

"Hey!" he called, "Shouldn't you be in the orchard with your little ones? Get back there at once!"

"But we haven't left them alone," said one cow. "Myrtle is with them. She wants to earn some extra money so she can buy herself a motorbike."

The farmer scratched his head. Whoever heard of a cow riding a motorbike? It was time to have a word with Myrtle.

Sure enough, there she was in the field, just as the others had said. Clustered around her, listening to a story about three bears, were the calves, together with the ducks from the pond, the sheepdog, a rabbit and two magpies. The farmer could hardly believe his eyes.

"Well, I'll be!" exclaimed the farmer. "I guess Myrtle must really want this motorbike. She's never volunteered for work before. Maybe I can find her some other jobs to do."

So, for the next few weeks Myrtle was very busy. Not only did she babysit the calves, she saw the ducks across the road to the pond, chased the fox out of the yard when he got too close to the henhouse and woke up the cockerel in the morning because he always overslept.

The farmer was impressed, and in no time at all she had saved up enough money. She could hardly wait to buy herself a shiny, new motorbike.

One bright, sunny morning, the farmer called to Myrtle as she stood in her field munching grass. "I am going to the market this morning. I can drop you at the motorbike showroom if you like."

Myrtle didn't need to be asked twice!

She rushed into the barn and picked up her purse with all her savings. She could barely contain her excitement as she clambered into the trailer that the farmer towed behind his tractor.

At last! She could picture herself roaring through the lanes with the wind rushing through her hair.

How jealous the other animals would be. She smirked to herself as she remembered how the chickens had laughed at her when she'd said she would buy a motorbike. Well, now she'd show them!

Myrtle walked into the showroom and gasped. She had never seen so many shapes, sizes and colours of motorbike all in one place.

She turned around and around until she was dizzy, but she knew all the time which one she wanted. It was in the corner by the window – all gleaming paintwork and the colour of the sky in July.

"Can I have that one, please?" she asked
the salesman, who was more than a little
surprised when he saw who his next
customer was. "And I would like a blue
helmet to match," she declared.

Myrtle danced around with glee as the farmer and the salesman loaded her shiny new bike into the trailer to take it back to the farm.

All the animals came to see as they drove into the yard – even the chickens who had mocked her so much.

She was so proud as the motorbike was wheeled out and parked in front of the farmhouse.

"Now, just you be careful," warned the farmer. "I don't want you hurtling around the yard causing an accident. Make sure you wear your gloves and helmet. Don't be so daft as to ride without them or I'll take it straight back to the showroom."

Myrtle couldn't bear the thought of her brand-new bike going back, so she promised the farmer she'd be careful.

She put on her helmet and pulled on her gloves. She could feel the excitement build in her as she sat astride the machine and switched on the engine. There was a splutter... then a hiccup... then a roar as the bike started.

Unfortunately, Myrtle was not as clever as she thought. Although the shiny new motorbike revved and roared its way across the farmyard, she stayed exactly where she was. Luckily, it skidded to a halt and fell over without causing any damage. Poor Myrtle felt so silly, sitting in the dust with her gloves and helmet on. How the animals laughed at her.

But Myrtle was determined to learn to ride her bike after she had worked so hard to get it.

Soon, the other animals lost interest and went back to their sheds or out to the fields. Only Tom the sheepdog remained, and he was used to teaching others. It was Tom who taught the sheep to run around obstacles and into pens at the Sheepdog Trials, although it was the farmer who took the credit.

Tom felt sorry for poor Myrtle because he knew how hard she had worked to save the money. He called out to her: "Myrtle, I've got an idea. Let me teach you to ride your motorbike. We can go into the orchard and ride between the trees."

He had seen people riding in and out of bright orange cones on the television in the farmhouse.

When they got to the orchard, they realised the ground was too rough, and poor Myrtle kept falling off.

"Oh, I shall never get the hang of this," she wailed in despair. "I may as well give up and take it back to the shop."

Tom was not about to let her give in that easily. He had an idea to help Myrtle to learn. He went to see the pigs to ask for their help.

Just behind the pigsty there was a stack of straw bales. Tom's plan was to build a course in the yard for Myrtle to practise on. The pigs helped him to arrange the bales to make a track for her.

On her first circuit, Myrtle got round without making a single mistake.

But the second time... oh dear! She drove around a corner much too fast, sending the chickens clucking for cover as she went through the bales. And then she went through the hedge and onto the road!

The pigs squealed in delight; they hadn't seen anything this funny since the farmer's daughter had fallen off her pony into the muddy pigsty.

Myrtle was hurtling down the road out of control. She frantically waved a hoof to signal to people to get out of her way.

Tom hadn't told her how to stop and now she was roaring towards the Vicar on his bicycle. He threw the bike to the ground and leapt over the wall into the churchyard for safety.

Still Myrtle hurtled down the road.

"Aaaagh!" she shrieked as the village pond came into view. But it was too late to do anything about it. Myrtle came to a wet, spluttering halt in the water, the ducks quacking and flapping in dismay. Frogs scattered in all directions, their peaceful afternoon shattered.

The farmer had heard the commotion and came trundling along in his tractor. He took one look at Myrtle with pondweed dangling from her helmet and laughed and laughed and laughed.

He helped her clamber out of the pond and they dragged the shiny new motorbike up onto his trailer.

He took it back to the showroom and got Myrtle her money back. Well most of it, it did need a good clean first.

She thanked him, deciding that perhaps a motorbike hadn't been such a good idea. What Myrtle thought she really needed was . . . a hang-glider!

Myrtle's Hang-Glider

"It's no good, Myrtle," said the farmer, "I can't afford to lend you the money to buy a hang-glider."

Myrtle turned and wandered sadly back to the field. Although she had money back when she returned her motorbike to the shop, it wasn't enough. Even if she worked twice as hard as before she would be at least a hundred years old before she could earn the amount she needed.

Tom the Sheepdog racked his brains to think of a way to make more money but nothing came to him.

Two days later the farmer was in the yard when the tanker from DairyCo Dairies arrived to collect the milk. The driver looked across the orchard to the field where Myrtle stood in the corner, looking glum.

"Why, Farmer, what's wrong with young Myrtle? She's usually so busy and full of life, yet she looks as though she has lost a pound and found a penny," he said.

"Oh," replied the farmer, "I'm afraid she's upset because I can't afford to buy her a hang-glider."

"Dear, oh dear, poor Myrtle," the driver said sympathetically. "I wish there was something I could do to help."

He connected the big pipe from the lorry to the dairy and listened thoughtfully as the milk gurgled and burbled through it and into his tanker. An idea struck him, but he decided not to say anything to the farmer just yet.

When he returned the next day the driver was not alone. He was with a smart-looking man in spectacles and a grey suit. The farmer was curious and walked across the yard to talk to him.

"Good morning," said the man in the suit, "I am the manager of DairyCo Dairies. I think

I may be able to help with your little problem."

Myrtle looked up from her corner of the field and saw the three men disappearing into the farmhouse. "I wonder what's going on," she said to herself.

An hour later the three men emerged from the farmhouse. The farmer shook hands with the manager and he got into the lorry.

"Goodbye," he said. "We will see you again soon." The driver waved cheerily to Myrtle as they pulled out of the yard.

All that day the farmer went around with a big grin on his face. Try as hard as they might, none of the animals could find out what was going on, not even Tom.

"I haven't the faintest idea," he said. "I expect we will find out soon, though."

At ten o'clock the next morning, a different lorry appeared at the farm. This also had DairyCo Dairies on the side, but it was big and square and didn't have a large silver pipe at the back.

The farmer called all the animals together. Even Myrtle forgot to be miserable in her rush to find out what was happening.

The man in the suit got down from the cab of the lorry and exchanged glances and a knowing smile with the farmer. They walked to the back of the lorry and opened the doors. The animals gasped in astonishment as they looked inside.

"What is it?" asked the littlest piglet, jumping up and down trying to look in the lorry.

First came something that looked like a small motor, then a harness appeared. Myrtle craned her neck to get a better view as they placed the final item on the ground.

"It's a tent," cried the pigs.

"No, it's a kite," squawked the chickens.

"Don't be silly," said Tom the sheepdog. "It's neither a tent nor a kite. It's the hang-glider that Myrtle wanted, and that motor will power it."

Myrtle nearly fell over in shock and surprise. She looked at the farmer, then at the man in the suit, then at the farmer again.

"Is Tom right? Is it really the hang-glider I wanted so much?"

The farmer laughed. "That's right, Myrtle. The manager of DairyCo Dairies has agreed to let you have the hang-glider for the same price as you paid for your motorbike. He said we could have it if he could paint DairyCo Dairies on the wings for everyone to see."

There was another man at the back of the lorry who showed Myrtle and the farmer how to attach the motor and the harness to the glider. When he was satisfied they knew what to do, he climbed back into the cab and shut the door.

"Goodbye!" he said. "Be careful up there, Myrtle, and have fun."

Myrtle turned to the manager and thanked him. "I'm so pleased. I never thought I could have a hang-glider after the farmer said he couldn't afford one."

"Think nothing of it," smiled the manager. "Although you really should thank the driver, he came into my office and suggested it. DairyCo Dairies are only too happy to help our customers whenever we can."

With that, the driver started the engine and they drove away, leaving the animals cheering and waving as they left.

Myrtle was so excited. She pleaded with the farmer to help her into the harness so she could try out her new hang-glider.

"I can't wait to have a go!" she cried. "Please, please will you help me?"

He needed to get on with the feeding and mucking-out, but he didn't have the heart to disappoint her.

They carried the glider into a big field to give her plenty of room. The other animals followed to watch her.

Soon she was all set up and ready to go. She put on her crash helmet, stood up, held onto the metal bar suspended underneath the hang-glider, and she ran... and she ran... and she ran. She ran from one end of the field to the other as fast as she could, but her hooves remained firmly on the grass.

How was she going to get off the ground?

It was Tom who saved the day. "What you need," he explained, "is to be high up before you try to fly."

"But how can I get high up if I can't get off the ground?" Myrtle was puzzled.

"Follow me." Tom led her back across the field, into the yard, and behind the barn.

"That's how." Tom pointed at the heap of grass piled up in the silage pit. It was covered in black plastic and was used to feed the animals in winter. It sloped steeply up towards the roof of the cowshed, where the cows lived in cold weather.

"All you have to do," smiled Tom, "is climb onto the roof and then jump off."

Myrtle gulped. It was a long way from the ground. But then, wouldn't she be even further from the ground when she was flying? She took a deep breath and did as Tom suggested.

Two pigs helped carry the hang-glider up the slope of the silage as Myrtle scrambled over the slippery black plastic and onto the roof of the cowshed. They let go as she teetered on the edge, preparing to jump.

"I wouldn't go up there without a parachute," said one pig.

"It's too dangerous to go up so high without some safety thing," said the other. "It's just as well Myrtle has got a hang-glider. At least she won't hit the ground so hard," said the first pig, nervously.

They slipped and slithered back down to the safety of the yard and looked up just in time. Myrtle checked her harness, started the motor, took a deep breath, and stepped into thin air.

The animals gasped.

She was flying!

Myrtle the cow was actually flying!

Higher and higher she went, just missing the farmhouse chimney as she flew over. "Whoops, that was close!" she giggled.

Myrtle looked down. The animals looked like tiny toys on a child's play-mat. Even the houses seemed to be small enough to step on. She flew over the fields and above the village. The church was below her and she could see where a few slates were missing from the roof.

I must remember to tell the Vicar about that when I see him next. Myrtle thought as she glided across the churchyard.

People playing cricket on the village green by the duck pond looked up in amazement as Myrtle whirred overhead. She remembered with a smile how she had ridden her motorbike into that pond. It had seemed so big then, but now it was just a saucer-sized puddle far below her.

A rook cawed in surprise as she waved at him flying past. How on earth did a cow get up here?

"What are you doing? Cows aren't supposed to fly, you know," he yelled crossly.

"Sorry," she said, "but this one can!"

An aeroplane roared above Myrtle, startling her. But the passengers in the plane were far more startled than she was. They pointed and giggled, making faces through the windows. What a tale they would have to tell when they landed!

Now Myrtle was flying over the town. She had never seen so many houses and streets before. Tall chimneys were dotted here and there. Myrtle coughed and spluttered as she flew through clouds of smoke.

"I don't like this bit!" She had tears streaming from her eyes. She would be glad when she had passed over the town and reached the countryside again.

Suddenly, down below, the land stopped. There were no more trees and houses, no more fields or roads. All there was, as far as the eye could see, was water. Myrtle gazed at it shimmering and sparkling in the sun.

"So that's what the sea looks like." She had never seen the sea before, only heard about it from the seagulls who followed the tractor when the farmer was ploughing the fields.

Myrtle decided it was probably time to go home. She couldn't see any land and she didn't know where the sea stopped. She carefully turned her hang-glider around, just as the man had told her, and headed for the farm.

The children were coming out of the school, running to their parents in the crowded playground.

"Look," cried a little girl, "I can see a flying cow!"

"Don't be silly," said her brother, "everyone knows cows can't fly."

Myrtle chuckled to herself as she made her way back to her field. Having decided on the best place to land she concentrated hard, trying to remember her instructions.

"It's Myrtle! It's Myrtle!" cried the other cows as she came to a sudden and uncomfortable stop in the hedge.

"Ouch!"

Her voice was muffled by brambles and she had scratches all over her. Luckily, the crash helmet had protected her head. She was very glad she had it on, that was certain!

Tom woke from his snooze under an apple tree and rushed off to get the farmer.

They came running through the field to help Myrtle out of her harness.

"The things I saw," she puffed, out of breath from the rough landing. "I saw the church, and the town, and the factories, and the pond. But, best of all, I saw the sea!"

"I remember going to the seaside when I was a pup," said Tom. "The farmer took me once on a daytrip. It's very big, isn't it?"

"Yes," agreed Myrtle. "That's why I decided to turn around and come home. I didn't want to run out of fuel and end up in the middle of it!"

The animals hurried to the field to listen to her tell them all about her adventures. They laughed when she described the astonished expressions on the faces of the people in the aeroplane.

"I love hang-gliding!" declared Myrtle. "And it's all thanks to the tanker driver and the lovely man from DairyCo Dairies."

"Yes," said the farmer, coming to help her pack the hang-glider away. "You must make sure you thank them when they come tomorrow."

The next day, the two men from Dairyco Dairies came back to find out how Myrtle had got on. The manager had a posh camera with him.

"I want to take a photo of you with the hang-glider," he said. "We want something new to paint on all our lorries, and I think a hang-gliding cow is just the thing!"

Myrtle posed for some photos then waved goodbye. "Thank you so much for helping me to fly!" she shouted as the lorry drove out of the yard.

Imagine how she felt a few weeks later when the new DairyCo tanker came to the farm. There it was, with a picture of Myrtle the Hang-gliding Cow smiling down from the side of it. That was almost as good as flying, and people all over the local area would see it!

Water-skiing, Myrtle?

"Water-skiing? Are you mad, Myrtle?" The farmer looked at her as if she was completely round the twist. "How on earth do you expect to go water-skiing? We live on a farm."

Myrtle walked away sadly. She thought the farmer could have been a little more enthusiastic. She knew exactly how she would do it, but she couldn't do it on her own. She might be able to ride a motorbike or fly a hang-glider (well, maybe not the motorbike) but there was no way she could drive a Land Rover at the same time as water-skiing. And she needed the Land Rover to pull her along.

Her plan was to persuade the farmer to pull her along in the river. One of his fields was on the riverbank – all he had to do was drive in a straight line. Myrtle would hold on to a rope attached to the back and she could ski across the surface of the water. Easy peasy.

One problem she hadn't foreseen was that she would sink as soon as she put her hooves in the water. Her friend Daisy had accidently fallen in a ditch last year and the farmer had to get his tractor to pull her out. She'd sunk quickly and even though it only came up to her tummy she couldn't get out by herself, no matter how hard she tried.

The farmer chuckled to himself as he tried to picture Myrtle on water-skis. He'd never come across a cow like Myrtle before. She was always thinking up crazy ideas and going on adventures. He supposed it was possible to tow her along behind his Land Rover, but he really was too busy.

"It's the middle of summer, and I have to cut and bale the hay and stack it in the barn ready for the winter. Maybe I can help you in a few weeks," he said.

Tom wanted to know why Myrtle was in such a bad mood. She told him about her plans to be the first cow on water-skis and how the farmer had spoilt her fun.

Tom gently pointed out that cows' hooves are not designed to walk on water, not even the ducks could do that. She would need something to help her stay afloat. Skis wouldn't work as she had too many legs. She would get in such a tangle if she had long pieces of wood strapped to each hoof.

"But what if I had one large piece of wood, Tom?" she asked. "Then I could stand on it with all four hooves."

"Don't be silly, Myrtle. A piece of wood big enough for you to stand on would be too heavy. It would sink before you got even one hoof on it, never mind all four. You need something lighter than that." Tom thought for a moment. "How about a polystyrene surfboard? I think there is one in the shed by the old stable block."

Myrtle got excited. Maybe if she could show the farmer she had thought it all out and planned every detail, he would agree to letting her try her idea.

She followed Tom to the shed, although it was quite a tight squeeze getting in through the narrow doorway. "I'll have to reverse out because there's no room to turn around," she complained.

Tom rummaged around and found the surfboard. It was battered and dusty but it should do the job. Secretly even he thought Myrtle had gone completely potty this time, but he didn't have the heart to upset her. He thought once she had a thorough soaking she would give up on the idea.

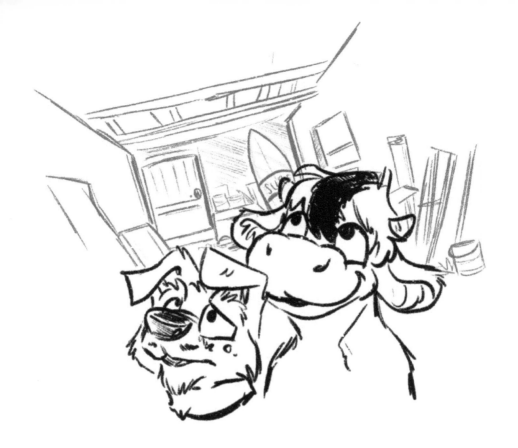

"Can you swim, Myrtle? I mean, have you ever been in water deeper than ankle-height?" He was sure the thought of being in water up to her ears would change her mind. "Can you float, at least?"

"I've thought of that, Tom," Myrtle said indignantly. She was beginning to think her friend wasn't as enthusiastic as he pretended to be. "I've heard of a coat you can wear to stop you from sinking and drowning. All I have to do is get one of those and everything will be fine."

"A coat to stop you sinking?" Tom was mystified for a moment, then it dawned on him. "Oh, I know what you mean, a lifejacket. But where are you going to get one from?"

"I've thought of that, too," Myrtle said triumphantly. "Mr Martin down by the Post Office has got a motorboat. He's bound to have some kind of lifejacket I can borrow. Will you come with me to ask him, please, Tom?"

Tom could see that nothing would change her mind so he decided he had better go along with her to make sure everything was all right. He had to run out of the yard as Myrtle had already backed out of the shed and was trotting down the road.

The people in the Post Office queue stared in surprise as Myrtle the cow hurtled past, closely followed by Tom the sheepdog. They thought perhaps she had escaped and the farmer had sent Tom to get her back.

How surprised would they be if they knew the truth? That she was intent on going water-skiing!

Mr Martin was in his driveway cleaning his car. He looked up as a breathless Myrtle skidded to a halt at his gate. She puffed and panted for a moment to catch her breath.

"Please, Mr Martin, can I borrow a lifejacket? I want to go water-skiing but I can't swim. I promise I will take care of it," she pleaded.

"Well, that's a new one on me and no mistake," laughed Mr Martin. "I can't say I've ever heard of such a thing before. Still, I suppose there's no reason why you can't give it a go. Of course you can borrow my lifejacket. I'll lend you my daughter's armbands too, just to be on the safe side."

Myrtle found it difficult carrying everything, so she decided the best solution would be to wear it.

Once again, the people in the Post Office stopped and stared as she went past. Poor Mrs Wilkins was so amazed she completely forgot her pension and went home without it. It wasn't every day you saw a cow walking up the road wearing a lifejacket and armbands!

Back at the farm, the farmer was wondering where his cow and his sheepdog had gone. "They're bound to be plotting some new scheme or other. I just hope it won't be dangerous and they'll be back before dark."

He was just about to drive his tractor out of the gate to work in one of the fields when Tom turned up, followed by a strange vision that caused the farmer to fall out of his tractor. Myrtle was such a sight in her orange lifejacket and red armbands.

"What are you playing at, Myrtle?" he cried, getting up and dusting himself off. "Have you lost your marbles completely?"

"Mr Martin said I could borrow these to go water-skiing," she explained. "I thought if you saw I had all the safety equipment you might agree to help me. All you have to do is drive the Land Rover along the riverbank with a rope attached. I'll do the rest." She gazed at him with her big cow-eyes and fluttering eyelashes, "Pleeeeeease?"

The farmer realised he would get no peace until he agreed to her madcap idea, so he said he would help her on the condition she waited until he had finished unloading the hay bales from the trailer into the barn.

Myrtle jumped up and down with excitement and pushed him back into the tractor, shutting the door behind him.

"Hurry up, then!" she said.

About an hour later they assembled in the field next to the river. A length of strong rope was tied firmly to the bumper of the Land Rover and attached to the surfboard. Myrtle pushed the board into the water to test it floated, then she climbed gingerly down the bank.

The farmer started the engine and leaned out of the window so he could see what was going on behind him. "Steady, now!" he called.

Myrtle had one hoof on the surfboard, two on the riverbank, and the other in mid-air over the glistening surface of the water. She hesitated for a moment, steadied the board with her hoof, then launched herself into the river. Tom signalled to the farmer, who drove as fast as he could. Tom raced after the Land Rover excitedly; he loved chasing cars.

The surfboard skimmed across the water like a skater on ice. But it was too close to the bank and Myrtle hit the side. It bounced into the air, landing in the field next to Tom. He yelped and jumped sideways to avoid being flattened. "Oi, watch out!" he shouted.

But what of Myrtle?

"Help! I'm all wet and soggy," she complained sadly.

She was bobbing around in the river, supported by her life jacket and armbands. She had come off the board as it flipped into the air, but she hadn't landed on the grass. Perhaps her idea to use the Land Rover hadn't been such a good one. She would have to think of something else instead. She was determined to be the world's first water-skiing cow.

The farmer helped her out of the river and back onto dry land. "Come on, Myrtle, soon have you nice and dry."

He refused to try towing her again and hoisted the board up into the back of his Land Rover before driving home, leaving Tom and Myrtle to walk.

"I'm not giving up yet, Tom," cried Myrtle. "But what am I going to do if the farmer won't help me any more?"

"Simple!" Tom replied. "You don't think Mr Martin keeps a lifejacket in case his livingroom gets flooded during a thunderstorm, do you? In case you had forgotten, he does have a motorboat. That's why he has a lifejacket. All we have to do is ask him if he would use his boat to help you become the first cow on water-skis."

Poor Mr Martin. He was astonished to see a dripping Myrtle standing in his front garden, still wearing the lifejacket and armbands. He listened as she described her failed attempt.

"Please, Mr Martin, can we borrow your motorboat?" begged the sodden cow.

Well, how could he refuse such a plea from the heart? They arranged to meet up the next day and Mr Martin went inside to ring the farmer.

"I've said I will help Myrtle and take her out in my boat in the morning, if that's OK with you?" he said.

"Anything to stop her nagging me!" chuckled the farmer.

The following morning, Myrtle clambered into the horsebox behind the tractor. They met Mr Martin at the beach so she could go water-skiing in the sea. The boat was already bobbing around in the water. Myrtle scrambled down the sand dunes as fast as she could.

"I'm here, Mr Martin!" She was beyond excited.

Soon she was dressed in lifejacket and armbands and a pair of goggles in case the water splashed in her face. As she put on her crash helmet, Mr Martin started the boat. The rope stretched tight and Myrtle got ready to hit the water.

A crowd had gathered on the beach to watch as Myrtle got closer and closer to the water's edge.

"She's not really going to do it, is she?" asked one man.

The next minute she was hurtling across the surface of the sea behind the boat. A huge cheer went up. A cow was waterskiing right in front of their eyes!

The people on the beach looked smaller and smaller as the boat went further out to sea. Myrtle could feel the wind rushing past her and taste the salty spray on her tongue.

"Wheee! This is fun!" She couldn't believe how fast she was going. Then she heard a squawk of surprise.

"Is that you, Myrtle? What on earth are you doing so far from the farm?" It was one of the seagulls that often followed behind the tractor.

"Hello," she replied, "I wanted to try water-skiing and managed to persuade Mr Martin to bring me out today. It's so exciting! I've never moved this fast in my life."

"Well, have fun," he said as he flew off towards the cliffs where the other seagulls were watching Myrtle with beaks wide open in astonishment.

A pod of dolphins raced alongside her, leaping out of the water, chirping and squeaking encouragement. They weren't quite sure what type of animal Myrtle was, but could see that she was enjoying herself.

Myrtle was ecstatic! Mr Martin turned the boat around and headed towards a small cove at the other end of the beach. The sea was calmer here and she didn't bounce around as much in the waves.

Mr Martin signalled to her that he wanted to stop in the cove for a while. The rope slackened as he slowed the boat so Myrtle came to a halt as her skis touched the soft sand.

"Wow!" she exclaimed. "I saw the sea from above when I was hang-gliding. I didn't think it could be so much fun being in it!"

Mr Martin laughed. "I could see you were enjoying yourself, but I wanted to stop for my lunch. Here, I brought some hay for you in case you were hungry."

"Thank you, I am a bit." She sat on the sand and took off her crash helmet to eat.

As Myrtle ate she looked around the beach. It was quite rocky, and she could see pools of water. Curious, she wandered off to have a look. Peering in the rockpools she saw green weeds, pink shells and tiny silvery fish. She bent down for a closer look.

"Ow!" Myrtle yelped as something pinched her nose, hard. "Why did you do that? It really hurt!"

"Why did you poke your great big nose into my home?" said the large and very grumpy crab that was hanging from the tip of Myrtle's nose.

"I was just looking, I didn't know you lived in the rockpool. Please will you let go, my nose is sore now."

"Sorry," The crab let go and plopped back into the water, disappearing under a stone.

"Myrtle! Time to go back now!" Mr Martin called from his boat.

She ambled back down to the shore, rubbing the end of her poor pinched nose. She put her crash helmet back on and carefully did up the strap. A sore snout was one thing, but she wasn't about to risk a bang on the head if she fell off the skis on the way back!

Mr Martin started the engine and they roared off towards the beach, Myrtle hurtling along behind him.

"Whoa! Aargh! Oo-er!" Myrtle clung on to the handle of the rope for dear life. The sea was rougher now because the tide was coming in fast. She gritted her teeth as the boat came to a halt on the sand.

"Look out!" A crowd of holidaymakers scattered as Myrtle hit the beach. Literally.

She let go of the rope and nearly flew over the front of the boat. Her skis came off and went in different directions, narrowly missing a picnic laid out on a tartan blanket.

"Oh heck! Ooof!" Myrtle somersaulted twice before landing in an undignified heap in front of the photographer from the local newspaper. She landed on her head and fell to the floor with a face full of sand.

"Steady on, Myrtle," said the photographer as he bent down to help her get up. "Don't worry, we won't print that one!"

"Thank you." She straightened her helmet and shook the sand from her face. She was so glad the farmer had insisted she wore it. She would probably have a big bump on her head if he hadn't.

Myrtle posed for a few more photos beside the boat before the farmer arrived with his Land Rover to take her home. She was glad to see him and Tom walking towards her. All the excitement had worn her out!

"Hello, Tom. I did it! I water-skied!"

"Well done Myrtle!" said Tom. "Let's get you in the Land Rover so we can all go home. You must be tired after all that."

Tom was right, Myrtle was exhausted. She climbed up into the back and settled down, making herself comfortable. She yawned and closed her eyes, smiling to herself happily. She was soon asleep and snored gently all the way back to the farm.

9 781789 422542